Sin Eater: A Ministry of Suffering

Isaac DeLuca

Sin Eater: A Ministry of Suffering

by Isaac DeLuca

Copyright © 2005

Lulu Enterprises, Inc.

Leviticus 16

20 And when he hath made an end of reconciling the holy *place*, and the tabernacle of the congregation, and the altar, he shall bring the live goat:

21 And Aaron shall lay both his hands upon the head of the live goat, and confess over him all the iniquities of the children of Israel, and all their transgressions in all their sins, putting them upon the head of the goat, and shall send *him* away by the hand of a fit man into the wilderness:

22 And the goat shall bear upon him all their iniquities unto a land not inhabited: and he shall let go the goat in the wilderness.

Becoming the Sin eater

Many Christians struggle daily with this world of suffering. There are many times in the life of all good Christians when we have opportunities to ease the passage of others through this life. We donate to charities, we volunteer our time to good organizations, and a great multitude of other worthy endeavors that we undertake as we spread the message of Jesus Christ. Though some of us find ourselves wondering if what we do is enough. There are those of us endowed with an awareness that sets us apart from our bretheren. There are those who find themselves endowed with unique sensitivities and powers that other members of their community do not possess. There are Christians who have a special gift, a certain sensitivity to the world and those around them. Unfortunately in a conventional church setting this gift is often shunned or suppressed because the Christian is afraid that the other members of the congregation or minister will look down upon them for having such a gift. In the Christian faith magic or

witchcraft of any kind is generally seen as the work of demons and
Lucifer, and as a result those Christians who have "special"
abilities are forced into hiding, or at the least to suppress their
natural gifts. Often as a result of their forced secrecy these people
turn away from the church, and some even turn their backs on the
Lord. If you are reading this text it is very likely that this is an
accurate description of the troubles with which you must contend.

I am here to tell you, DO NOT BE AFRAID. There is still a
place for you in the Christian faith, one with a rich history and a
vibrant modern tradition. There is a role that you can assume
within the faith that may very well be suited to your unique gifts.
This is not magic, it is a ministry. This is not witchcraft, it is a way
of life. You can become a sin eater.

A sin eater is a person who has the capacity to sense, draw
out, and consume the suffering of others. For what thing more
than suffering is the root of sin? Gluttony. Avarice. Lust. Envy.
Pride. Sloth. Wrath. All of these sins and many more are the result
of suffering. Though only through Jesus can anyone hope for

salvation, the sin eater takes upon himself the suffering in the

hopes that the unburdened soul can find its way back to the Lord.

This book is a guide to those who would become such a person,

and serves as a manual for a successful ministry as a sin eater.

The Sin Eater in History

Most mythology and folklore paints a picture of the sin eater as a pathetic and ill-favored individual. Folklore from Wales, and later in American Appalachia, presents sin eating as a burial custom. According to folklore the sin eater was a person who lived alone deep in the countryside and was avoided by everyone, for he was so permeated with the transgressions of others that he was someone to be kept at a distance. When a person was dying or deceased, a representative would be send into the countryside to fetch the sin eater. Then this wretch would journey to the home of the deceased or dying and place certain items near or upon the person. Sometimes bread and cheese was used, other times a bowl of crude ale or gruel would be employed. The sin eater would then consume this ritual mean, and as a result of this would take upon himself all of the transgressions of the deceased, allowing them to pass into the gates of Heaven. The sin eater would then be given a pittance wage of coin and driven from the village. Sometimes this ejection from civilization was symbolic, other times it was quite literal. In other cultures the sin eater was simply a poor person forced, for a small wage, to sit next to the corpse of the recently deceased and consume a meal, and held no special place in society. Other forms of this sort of practice can be found throughout history and culture, from the 'death sitters' of rural America to the 'demon eaters' of more Eastern cultures. Though modern sin eating has it's roots in the traditions of the death sitters and sin eaters from folklore, the modern ministry of suffering is not limited by superstition or the arrival of death.

The Basics

There are a multitude of books, tapes, workshops, and articles that focus on what are considered to be the basics of interpersonal Christian ministry. As such, there will be no exhaustive discourse on these elements. However, there are three basic aspects of faith-based esoteric practice that are of great importance to the understanding and capacity to interact with the concepts presented in this text, and pursuant to this will be presented in a limited fashion here. These basic elements are physical fitness, meditation, and energy manipulation.

Despite how much we may or may not view the flesh as a prison, after a Gnostic Christian fashion, we are beings housed in and a part of the physical realm. Keeping the body, this temple, at peak condition is important to any ministry endeavor. When the body is good physical condition there is an abundance of vitality, awareness, and endurance, all of which are important faculties as a sin eater. This is best done through balanced diet, consistent exercise, uninterrupted restful sleep, and good personal hygiene. When the body is well rested as a result of sleep, full of vitality as a result of a balanced diet, refreshed by cleanliness, and poised from exercise, the sin eater is ready to engage in effective ministry. Not only will these healthy habits improve the quality of your life, but also the potency, duration, and precision of your ministry.

Meditation is a cornerstone of esoteric practice, though is not as rigid as one might think. There are a multitude of theories and methods of meditation, in fact, it is not the act of meditation that is of importance, and it is the resulting state of relaxed readiness that is the goal. The most simple meditation technique is to find a comfortable physical position, though not one that will encourage the practitioner to fall asleep unexpectedly (hence the common usage of an upright or sitting position). Once in place, the practitioner begins to breathe deeply, not hyperventilating, but drawing breath all the way down into the lower parts of the lung, and breathing out in a controlled and slow manner. Eventually the mind will sharpen and the body will relax, creating the ideal state of relaxed readiness. It is from this state of relaxed readiness that effective ministry springs forth. In time the sin eater will become adept at achieving this R&R state with a single controlled breath, allowing them to prepare for empowered action at a moment's notice.

Energy manipulation, like fitness and meditation, is discussed at length in many texts and sources external to this book, though a brief overview will be given. Many cultures worldwide have their own terms, explainations, and traditions surrounding the unseen energies of the world. Some Eastern traditions, by far the most widely known to Westerners, call the energy of life 'chi' or 'ki'. They become intimate and skilled in it's manipulation, becoming capable of 'spiritual surgery' and incredible feats of endurance and strength. They tend to think of this energy as simply the energy of life, a bio-field generated by all living things. This notion is very similar to the Hindu views of what they call 'prana'. However, the concept of energy work is not monopolized by just Buddhists and Hindu, the Jewish mystics who practice the Kabbalah also utilize

an energy tradition. For Jewish mystics, a fundamental element o their tradition is the 'raising of the divine spark', a notion of a spiritual energy of a divine nature, that through the spiritual work and contemplation of the mystic must be empowered to return to the Lord. Even the tribal cultures of the Native Americans have within their belief systems an energy tradition. Hunters and shamans would make a mental and spiritual effort to achieve a 'hollow state', in which one's spiritual being is like the autumn reed, so that the energies that need to be channeled can have an uniterupted flow. Thus the hunter can become more like the deer which he is stalking, and the shaman can embody the animal spirit he is attempting to contact.

Though all of the above examples are Non-Christian, and thus not the best path for the sin eater, it is important to study the theory and general assumptions about reality that form the foundations of such traditions. Throughout history the Christian faith has been somewhat suscpicious, to say the least, of energy traditions and esoteric spiritual work. An advantage placed at the feet of the modern sin eater is the luxury of being able to practice your ministry somewhat in the open, without fear of death or injury. Though you may find yourself in many a theological debate, it is unlikely you will find yourself in any physical danger. In this more tolerant age, the Christian minister has the opportunity to study the energy traditions of other cultures, not to convert to them, but to study their inner workings. Misguided as they may be, most energy traditions have been in existence since before the coming of Christ, and have had a great deal of time to evolve. As a sin eater, it is best that you study these traditions in order to gain a better understanding of energy work than this slim tome can offer. So long as you stay true to your faith, you can study these spiritual disciplines, and gain a mastery of meditation, biofeedback, and energy work that will allow you to become attuned to, and be able to interact with, this world of suffering.

Suffering energy, as the fundamental element of the sin eater's ministry, must be manipulated by the sin eater in order to manifest the transfer of suffering. There are a plethora of theories and techniques regarding energy manipulation, and it is likely that

the reader of this book is already well versed, or at least familiar,

in such techniques, though some things bear repeating. Energy

must first be sensed, this can be done with a combination of the

'hyper-senses' which will be discussed later in the book and the act

of visualizing the energy you are being faced with in whatever

manner is most compatible with your personal faith. Once the

energy is sensed you must reach out with your will and take

control of that energy, shaping it into consumable patterns of your

choosing, or using the pre-existing patterns as you see fit. This is

the most basic element of the ministry of suffering, and is heavily

reliant upon the strength of your will and your faith. Once the

energy is shaped it can be transferred into the sin eater. When the

sin eater has consumed as much as he or she can bear, ground the

leftover energy by projecting it into either an object, the earth

itself, or dissipating it into the ambient environment. Naturally, the

most basic method is the energy strand. Simply draw upon the

suffering energy, shape it using visualization and your will, then infuse it with your intent and draw it into yourself, channeling the

suffering of one being into yourself through this visualized conduit

of energy.

Hyper-Senses

In order for a sin eater to become a dynamic force of salvation, that sin eater must have the ability to perceive the reality in which he or she is working. The aspiring sin eater must develop what can easily be called 'hyper-senses'. Much like sight, sound, taste, touch, and smell, these senses must be recognized and developed in order for the sin eater to be able to interact with and manifest the will within reality. These senses for the most part mirror the standard five senses, though some extend past those five and become what many people refer to as the sixth sense and beyond. This is the art of observation and perception.

How can a sin eater hope to interact with suffering if it cannot be sensed? How powerful can the changes wrought in reality be if the sin eater who manifests those changes cannot perceive the results of the exertion of her will? If a person is riddled with suffering and the sin eater does not have the hyper-senses necessary to notice, what hope has he or she of consuming it? These are the sorts of problems that a sin eater without developed magical senses can find themselves dealing with. The development and constant maintenance of these senses is of the utmost importance, because it is these senses that will allow the sin eater to observe and perceive during ministry situations and deal with them as they arise. A sin eater at the top of his game is proactive and preemptive, not blindly reactionary.

The most effective training method is a visualized expansion of awareness that in time becomes actual suffering awareness. First achieve a meditative state, either through personal meditation techniques or whatever mental or physical methods the individual uses to enter a state of calm. Once you have settled into this state, begin to expand your awareness. Try to visualize your room in your mind's eye, see without seeing. Now combine your other senses with this mental picture. Hear the room, and use the ambient sound to construct that same mental picture. Then create that picture with smell and taste. Try to create the picture with touch, this will require you to visualize your sense of touch extending far beyond your physical body. Imagine the textures of the various objects in the room, the walls, and the floor. Once you have created the picture in your mind, try to create it using all five of your senses at once. Sight will naturally come the most easily, but once you see the room try to hear it with your eyes open. Now, while watching and listening to the room, smell, taste, and touch it. The point of this exercise is to illustrate to the sin eater that even the common human senses can be used with much more detail, precision, and range when coupled with creative visualization.

After considerable practice expanding the five senses, now it is time to discover and develop the hyper-senses. For the most part hyper-senses are types of energy perception, a good metaphor would be that a sin eater who has developed hyper-senses can perceive not only suffering, but the very fabric of reality. The best way to begin training in these senses is to repeat the above exercises, though instead of perceiving the physical elements of the room, use sight, hearing, taste, touch, and smell to become aware of the energy patterns that make up the physicality of the room. It would be beneficial at this point to add a few religious items to the room, perhaps the sin eater's personal Bible or priest robes. For the most part the physical objects in the room will feel energetically just like they do with the standard senses. However, when perceiving religious items the sin eater will be able to hone the senses to an awareness of the subtle faith empowered properties of the items. At the most basic levels of skill the sin eater will be able to tell a faith charged item from a mundane item, be able to pick out the empowered Bible from an entire collection of Bibles for example. The more developed this sense becomes, the sin eater will be able to perceive what sorts of energies permeate the items, allowing the sin eater to divine elements of the item's origins and purpose. The more aware of energy patterns in reality the sin eater becomes, the better able she will be to interact with those elements of reality.

<u>Resonance</u>

When a sin eater gathers energy in a transfer of sin, one must remember that the energy is not going to be "pure". It will by all means be pure energy, but the energy itself with have what is called a resonance. It is this resonance, or flavor if you will, of the energy that will determine some of its unique qualities.

For example, if a sin eater happens upon a burial ground and performs the transfer upon the dead, the energy that he gathers will have the flavor of those burial grounds and the recently dead. Perhaps this visualization, energy could easily be seen metaphorically as water. Water is water, but water from any source will be different on some level than water from another source. There is distilled water, pond water, river water, ocean water, sewage, run off, and precipitation. Water tends to take on characteristics of its environment, so it is with energy. It is for this reason that a sin eater from a Catholic faith might find that her ministry feels different when permeated by energy from a

Protestant sinner than from members of her own congregation, or put more simply, the suffering of a murderer is different from that of a thief.

Think of the old cliché "you are what you eat". This very much applies to sin eaters in two major ways. The first is that sin eaters are more affected by the resonance of locations and suffering energy than normal people, and sustained exposure to such locations and energies affect sin eater. So the more attuned to a location, or certain type of suffering energy (guilt, wrath, fear, etc.) a sin eater is, the more it will "color" their ministry. More often than not sin eaters are easily identified by what sort of ministry they seem to be doing, the resonance of their energy.

It is this coloring of the ministry by the resonance of the suffering energy that is another way in which the resonance directly affects the sin eater herself. Think of the metaphor of the athlete. If a person trains constantly for running, they will develop the long and lean body type of a runner. If a person is a weight lifter or football player, they will develop the stocky body type that best fits their chosen sports. All sports are like this to some degree, with a certain body type being superior to all others in that particular sport. Now, what would happen to a runner who tried to enter a body building contest? Or a ballerina who suddenly had to play football?

This is what happens to sin eaters who allow themselves, for better or worse, to take on the resonance of a specific type of suffering energy. The more guilt-based suffering consumed, the more permeated with the guilt resonance the sin eater will become. The result is that they become an immaculate sin eater of guilt, but their abilities in dealing with murder or sickness might very well lessen. While it tends to be natural for sin eaters to become permeated to at least a moderate degree with one sort of suffering energy resonance, it can become detrimental to the flexibility of the sin eater to become trapped in one of these aspects. For example, a sin eater is incredibly powerful when he works with victims of domestic violence. Force him to work with the recently deceased, and his ministry will be in serious jeopardy.

Energy resonance can be garnered just about anywhere and doing any sort of ministry. It is no different for an itinerant sin eater. As a traveler the lone sin eater will have the ability to maintain a relatively clean slate when it comes to resonances from locations. Also, with a clear mind and a taste for variety the wanderer will be able to avoid a rut in the types of suffering consumed. Yet one must accept the fact that the lone sin eaters over time becomes permeated by the energy of solitude, which for some is also a kind of suffering. So travelers should take care that they stop sometimes. Pick a place to settle down for a few months, clean out your pipes so to speak. As said above, resonance permeation can make one incredibly powerful, but limits the sin eater who is trapped in that aspect. So in conclusion, be aware of your permeation levels. Make sure you get some variety in your ministry, but if you find something you like don't hesitate to focus upon it, just don't get trapped. The worst thing a sin eater can do is become so overloaded with suffering that one is dragged down with it. Always remember to take the time to speak with your minister if you feel yourself beginning to fall under the weight of your burden. Pray often, and even if you are not Catholic, the act of going to a priest and making confession is a powerful act, especially for a sin eater. You alone can only consume so much suffering before you are crushed under its weight, be aware of your limits. There will always be the temptation to try to heal the world on your own, but you must deny yourself that delusion. Only Jesus can save the world. It is your job to help as many burdened souls be free from their suffering so that they can open themselves to the Lord.

Ritual and Image

As human beings we are creatures of images. In our earliest times to the present we have been enamored of images. We make paintings on cave walls and carvings or statues of our gods and heroes. As we have expanded our range of mediums of imagery we seem to have become much more reliant upon external imagery than a translation of the internal to the external. In essence, we have lost or suppressed that inner imagery for favor of the easier and less committed imagery of the external. Instead of listening to the tales of our elders and contemplating our faith, we watch movies and play high-tech video games. It isn't that these more modern mediums of image expression are better or worse than those of the past, the problem is that these modern mediums have become so central that the old ways have been all but ousted. While the modern mediums are wonderful and deeply expressive and rich in visual qualities, they lack the deep internal commitment that contemplation and storytelling demand. In many ways we have pushed away our ability to visualize and express for ourselves internally, we have to have something tangible, like a movie or a magazine. For the sin eater visualization is not only a necessary talent, but also a cultivated skill.

Any action executed by a human being requires visualization on the part of the person. Even something as simple as reaching for a glass of water. The person visualizes a glass of water in their hand and so doing, reaches for the glass and picks it up. The same basic principle is at work in the sin eater's ministry. Once a sin eater has reached the point where they have ascended and no longer need visualization beyond the basics, executing a transfer of suffering energy is no more complicated than moving one's arm to collect a glass of water. However, for those of us who are not at that step a more complicated process of visualization is necessary. When a sin eater consumes there must be an internal visualization of what is going on around and inside them. Because ministry is normally an act whose effects and results tend to exist in the realm of the invisible the sin eater must visualize both its process and results. This visualization shapes the transfer and empowers it. Without any shame or reservation the sin eater must see internally through the imagination the channeling of the suffering, the shaping of it, and the consuming of it. For many this may be a sufficient amount of visualization, because their imaginations are vivid enough that they are able to create enough of a personally believable visualization that they consume the energy without many external clues as to what they are doing.

For many others however, simply visualizing consuming the suffering just isn't sufficient. This is the role of ritual in a sin eater's ministry. A ritual is any external process executed for the purpose of consuming suffering. Rituals can be as simple as lighting a candle or as complicated as month long purifications or choreographed movements and special words. The purpose of all ritual is to focus the sin eater's attention and power to a fine point. Ritual also provides a potent structure and shape for the energies being used by the sin eater. Here is an example: The reason the cross is such an important parts of the sin eater's ministry is that it is a very powerful conductor and receptacle of energy. Partly because of their relationships to Jesus crucified, but also the vast and potent cultural connotations. This is the cross upon which Jesus died for our sins. Also, due to our perception of those relationships we are more open in our hearts and minds to the fact that these items can be used in the sin eater's ministry. Many times these items are more powerful than many other things, as long as we have faith and make them so.

Methods of Ministry

Historically sin was transferred from the dead to a living sin eater through food, often bread, salt, or cheese laid upon the chest of the deceased then consumed by the sin eater. The role of the sin eater in a historical context was to deal almost exclusively with the recently deceased, ministering to the living is a relatively modern development. For the modern sin eater, one not bound by local superstition or custom, it is the personally relevant symbolism of the event that is of importance. You may choose to use a plate or tray to facilitate the transfer. If the sinner is still living, one would place the dish at the feet of the sinner. Then, like Jesus washing the feet of the Apostles, the sin eater would eat from this plate of food, taking in the subject's sins as your own. If the sinner is dead, then in this case perhaps tradition is best observed. Place the dish upon the chest or abdomen of the deceased, and eat from the plate.

The sin eater, by going through the ritualized placing of the dish and eating of the food, will transubstantiate the food into the sins and suffering of the subject. As you consume the food, so too are you fundamentally taking the sins of the subject into yourself.

Like the first breath of life into the lungs of Adam, so is every breath drawn by the living of extreme significance. Breathing is the vital process of life, and as such is one of the most potent symbols of our humanity. As this is such a fundamental element of being human, the sin eater is able to use the breath as a powerful tool for consuming suffering. Using your meditative techniques coupled with your hyper-senses to become aware of the breathing of your subject. Once you have become fully aware of the person's breathing, begin to physically match the opposite rhythm of your breathing to the subject's, so that when they breathe out you are breathing in. As your breathing becomes synchronized, begin to visualize the subject's suffering passing through their breath into yours. Each time they breathe out, you are coaxing forth their sins and breathing them into yourself. With each breath their suffering energy will be drawn into you. Once you have reached your capacity, end the situation with either physical contact or holding your breath. The physical contact could be something as impersonal as a casual shoulder to shoulder touch as you walk past, or as intimate as a light kiss on the forehead of the subject. If physical contact is not possible or appropriate, holding your breath as long as possible is a good way of shutting off the contact and returning your breathing to normal. The practice of taking suffering through the breath is the most common method used when dealing with the living, and serves as a gateway to the most advanced sin eater technique.

The greatest achievement of the sin eater's ministry is the moment the sin eater gains the ability to consume suffering from a distance at will. Once a familiarity with the energy of suffering is attained, the sin eater of sufficient faith will begin to understand the subtle and insidious complexities of that energy. By gaining and awareness of the ebb and flow of suffering, the sin eater will be able to reach out with his or her will, and consume it. This is the true level of mastery. Upon the realization and awareness of this energy, your mind will begin to reveal to you the awesome truth:

your ministry can be global. The limitations of your ministry are defined by the horizons of your awareness. If you can sense it, you can consume it.

Imagine for a moment, just how much suffering a lone sin eater could consume if he or she had the power to transfer suffering from across the globe. Conjure in your mind's eye a place of terror, sin, and suffering. Once you have this place, or situation, or group of people firmly held in your awareness, focus your will upon their energies. Upon reaching out and becoming aware of those energies, you have the ability to consume their sins from across the world. Using the breath methods mentioned above in conjunction with this global ministry is recommended, primarily because using your breath as a visualization for taking on the suffering of the world allows the sin eater to carefully regulate the amount of energy consumed. This power relies heavily upon your ability to master the basic sin eater skills of meditation and energy manipulation.

A World of Suffering

This world can be a dark place. It is full of suffering of all kinds. It is our duty as sin eaters, as Christians, to do everything in our power to make this world a better place. The ministry of suffering is a long and arduous path, and it is difficult for anyone to walk it alone. I encourage you to seek counsel with your minister or your priest. These people are servants of the Lord just as you are, and have a great deal of training in helping you to live your life well. Do not let the powers that you have go to your head, do not fall prey to hubris and pride. This is a gift, use it well.

The General Perennial Principles of Theurgy

In nearly every culture of the world there is, or once was, a notion of what is known today as theugry. Theurgy is the act of creating miracles, or magic, through the Grace of God. Theurgy IS NOT witchcraft, it is the channeling of divinity in order to create miracles, or events which would be described by witnesses as 'magic'. Word like 'magic' and 'esoteric' tend to have negative connotations for most Christians, and it should be said here and now that theurgy is not possible without faith. The words vary from culture to culture, but they all have the same general meaning, so for the sake of clarity the word theurgy will be used in all cases. Also, for the sake of time and clarity, the existence of theurgy will not be questioned in this text. It will be assumed, within the scope of this text, that theurgy does exist and the issue will not be addressed further.

From the past to the present theurgy has been a part of many, if not most, of the cultures of the world. Each culture has it's own views as to the properties, uses, and ethics of theurgy. With so many cultural versions it can be very difficult to gain a real understanding of theurgy. This has led to much of the skepticism of it throughout the years. Since the ideas of therugy are so varied throughout the world it has been difficult if not impossible for many to accept the validity of both science and theurgy. Many people are of the opinion that if science were to be integrated with the idea of theurgy in its many current forms, that science would be somehow lowering itself, the same could be said of some modern Christians and Christian institutions. In order for there to be an integration of the two disciplines in accordance with the Christian faith all therugy must be unified under one set of principles, much like science has its foundations in the scientific method.

In order to create this set of principles a perennial approach must be taken. Perennial philosophy is a way of thinking that takes into account one's own existence and experiences, but also those of all people past and present. It is a school of thought that attempts to find a commonality in human experience and understanding. The perennial approach would search out common ideas and views of therugy and put them together. In the perennial approach we try to find the commonalties of theurgy throughout the world. With these commonalties we will be able to identify the core elements of theurgy. From those core elements the classical principles of theurgy can be developed.

While making the attempt to create such a set of principles it is important to include absolutely no cultural elements in the principles. There are persons who would disagree with this; the argument being that culture is necessary and that stripping it away is foolish and disrespectful. The removal of culture from the set of principles is necessary to provide science with an unbiased and objective counterpart. Once theurgy and science are made to coexist then the culture surrounding theurgy can once again be considered because the basic principles that culture's theurgy is working off of have been identified, thus satisfying the demands of science.

There is an unfortunate lack of respect in the field of science towards the practice and existence of theurgy, just as there is an equal amount of aversion towards science in the minds and hearts of many who follow more religious paths. In our culture the importance of science has been elevated above all other things, many times at the expense of faith. Perhaps by taking up the practice of theurgy and entering into a dialogue with science these problems can be dealt with.

What follows is the set of principles I was able to identify and develop through my own research into the various theurgist traditions of the world, both past and present.

1. All energy is potential theurgist energy.

2. Theurgy is the use of will to elicit change in energy towards a desired end.

3. The ability to use theurgy is directly affected by belief.

4. The power of theurgy depends upon the focus of the user.

"All energy is potential theurgist energy."—This is the principle that shows homogeneity of energy in all theurgist traditions of the world. Most cultures have a word that is a close approximation of this divine energy. Some cultures call this energy "mana", others call it "chi", and some just call it "juice". There are many names for this divine energy that is believed by these cultures to permeate the world, and is there for those who can access it. The fact that every theurgist culture has some idea of a divine energy shows a commonality. Physics shows that all natural events involve a transformation of energy from one form to another, but the amount of energy does not change in the transformation. The law of conservation of energy shows us that matter and energy can neither be created nor destroyed. Albert Einstein showed that all matter is energy. If everything in creation is energy in some form, including the divine energy used by theurgists, and energy cannot be created or destroyed, only transformed, then it can be said that all energy is theurgist energy.

"Theurgy is the use of will to elicit change in energy towards a desired end."—This is the principle that deals with the actual act of theurgy. Of the four principles this is the one that is found in every culture almost without exception. Many cultures see theurgy

as an individual acting apart from society or religion in order to

achieve some personal goal, and when acting alone the only tool

one has is the will. The process of theurgy, the act of using one's

will to do theurgy, is morally neutral. The moral implications of

theurgy fall upon the shoulders of the theurgist, not the energy

itself. Through the use of will changes are made in energy, that,

provided the will is strong enough, result in the desired outcome.

Much like it takes will to pray or fast for hours on end, it takes will

to summon up energy and use it to cause changes in reality.

"The ability to use theurgy is directly affected by belief."—

This principle of theurgy is the principle what illustrates the

dynamic nature of theurgy. It can be inferred from this principle

that if a person does not believe in God or that they are capable of

theurgy then they are not capable of doing so. One might argue

that experiences like speaking in tounges, a phenomenon entailing

the abundant rising of potent spiritual energy from the base of the

spine, happens regardless of belief in theurgy. While speaking in tounges is a powerful experience, the person experiencing the

awakening is not at that moment willworking. The awakening

does however greatly encourage the belief in such things as more

energy openings occur in the person, which eventually develop

into faith-based powers like the laying of hands, which are in their

most basic, non-cultural nature, theurgy. The ability to use theurgy

is not only the capability of theurgy, but also the style of the

ability. The way in which one believes theurgy works greatly

shapes one's ability to use it. For instance, many Christian

exorcists believe that their powers come from studying texts and

religious rituals. Many of them even believe that their leaders and

celestial allies grant powers to them. They also believe that such

powers can be taken away from them. Many practitioners of faith

healing also believe that their powers are granted to them in some

form by the Lord. There are other theurgists who belong to a

group known as the Gnostics who believe that one's theurgical

ability is a measure of one's will, and that the only limiting factor

the self. If one strips culture away from this principle it can be seen that belief shapes the ability to use theurgy, which is a commonality among most cultures.

"The power of theurgy depends upon the focus of the user."—This principle is perhaps the most broad of the four principles. This principle deals with several elements of focus. One of the elements of focus is the ability of the theurgist to gather various amounts energy and shape it into the desired form without losing control of the summoned energy. An example of this would be a Catholic exorcist attempting to write scripture upon the wooden shaft of a crucifix. The more energy the priest puts into the writing of the lines of scripture, the more powerful they will become. If the excorcist tries to use more energy than he can control and still create the relic, then something undesirable might happen, such as the crucifix breaking or the scripture simply not working. Many people believe that this is one of the many roles played by rituals. Aside from their social functions, rituals provide the therugist with a specific way to go about using energy. Many psychologist and sociologist have shown that human beings like order. To be more specific, human beings like maps. The rituals

serve as maps for the theurgist to keep in mind while they work, it

is a tool for deepening one's concentration and energy controlling

capacity. Because of this many feel that ritual is a tool to be used

until the theurgist is capable of causing the same changes without

the use of ritual, metaphorical training wheels in a way. For these

traditions, the more internalized rituals become, the less one has

need for them. Though as Christians, certain symbols and rituals

are of vital importance to our faith, and cannot be discarded. The

other element of focus is the perceived source of the energy being

utilized by the theurgist, this is especially important for sin eaters.

Many theurgist focus on drawing the energy from within their own

being, in essence they see themselves as their own power source.

Others focus on drawing their energy from specific deities. This is

not to say that the above sort of focus applies to those people who

coerce spirits for aid. This focus applies to the practitioners of

theurgy. For theurgist, the energy that they use comes directly

through the deity that they are focusing upon. An example of this would be a Catholic priest performing an exorcism upon a

possessed person, by invoking the power of God the priest is able

to shape that power and use his will to cast the demon out.

Now that the principles have been shown and explained, one

might wonder why one would practice theurgy in the first place.

There are several reasons. One reason is responsibility. Each

person's responsibilities are different; therefore, they will need

different ways of dealing with those responsibilities. Ministers,

priests, police officers, and politicians perform their services to aid

and protect their societies. Parents are responsible to their

families. Citizens are responsible to their governments just as

governments are responsible to their citizens. Theurgy, just like

any other skill or tool, can help a person to live up to their

responsibilities. It is a potent addition to the versatility of

individuals who have theurgy as one of their abilities. In addition

to being a very useful skill or tool, theurgy has a deeper element to

its practice. Many of the theurgist traditions of the world see it as

a way of deep exploration of the self and the universe, and

ultimately God. When someone enters into the practice of theurgy that person comes into contact with very powerful forces within the universe that serve to deepen the theurgist's perceptions. The exposure to theurgy and divine energy forces a widening of one's sense of the universe. It shatters the construct of a purely rational and empirical worldview, and forces the person to live in a much wider, deeper, more cosmically aware state of being.

There is, however, a common pitfall that many people may experience in relation to the practice of theurgy. Theurgy is, as one can see from the four principles, a practice that can easily lead to the inflation of the ego of the theurgist. Grandiosity and egocentrism can be very difficult problems that sometimes develop in the lives of theurgists, both past and present. Some might begin to flaunt their powers before those without them. Others may interpret their powers as evidence that they are some sort of important religious figure, the "One". Many might make the mistake of placing will above all other things as what is best in people, this sentiment stemming from the use of will in theurgy of course. Sometimes the theurgist gets caught up in the power before the openings of perception occur and the deepening of the self becomes a reality. The struggle not to fall into egocentrism and grandiosity is an ongoing one, so vigilance and openness must always be maintained. You must maintain constant vigilance that your practice of theurgy does not stray from your faith. You are an instrument for God's will, once you begin to use your gifts for you own ends, you have strayed into hubris and witchcraft.

The Flagellant Processions

What I will attempt in this chapter to accomplish is to provide a potent, if somewhat misguided, example of a massive sin eater movement in history. Though they did not think of themselves in such explicit terms as 'sin-eaters', their story is one of high value to anyone considering the ministry of suffering. While this chapter has been included in the sin eater's manual, treat this as more of a parable. Examine this chapter closely, for it contains both the idealistic elements of the ministry of suffering, though also illustrates some of the pitfalls therein.

"shut himself up in his cell and stripped himself naked…and took his scourge with the sharp spikes, and beat himself on the body and on the arms and on the legs, till blood poured off him as from a man who has been cupped. One of the spikes on the scourge was bent crooked, like a hook, and whatever flesh it caught it tore off. He beat himself so hard that the scourge broke into three bits and the points flew against the wall. He stood there bleeding and gazed at himself. It was such a wretched sight that he was reminded in many ways of the appearance of the beloved Christ, when he was fearfully beaten. Out of pity for himself he began to weep bitterly. And he knelt down, naked and covered in blood, in the frosty air, and prayed to God to wipe out his sins from before his gentle eyes."   ---Cohn (127)

In the overcrowded and desolate cities and towns of medieval Italy a movement began, the flagellant procession. The movement had its foundations with a hermit of the city of Perugia in the year 1260, and the movement quickly spread south towards Rome and north towards Lombard. From that year on, until the late 1400's the flagellant movement was a powerful force in medieval Europe.

The flagellant processions of the medieval times were both frightening and inspirational. In essence, the flagellants were punishers of their own bodies. They would pierce, flog, and beat themselves both in public and in private. This was all done with the hope of convincing God to have mercy upon the people, and visit them with less suffering and death. They hoped that because of their acts of self-torture God would forgive them of their sins, gift them with salvation, and make the world that they presently lived in a somewhat better place.

The tortures that they inflicted against themselves were almost inhuman. Many flogged themselves with a type of whip called a scourge; it consisted of a handle with several leather strips hanging off of it. Each one of these leather strips had a twisted piece of metal fastened to the end of it so that when a person was struck the bits of metal would tear out flesh with each strike. Other punishments involved torturing each other with hot iron spikes, simply burning and piercing the flesh until the person collapsed. Some even carried life-sized crucifixes upon their backs, punishing themselves by carrying the heavy structure over the many hard miles that the processions covered on their journeys. Some simply tied themselves up with rope and had themselves beaten, or they would just beat themselves.

The processions moved about from city to city, resting where they could and publicly torturing themselves. They were usually lead by priests who had either given up on the church or had been forcibly removed from the church by their superiors. When the hordes of man and boys would arrive in a city they would march into the city bearing banners and burning candles. Once inside the city they would divide into groups and spread about the city, usually in front of local churches, and publicly punish themselves for hours at a time.

This public display of penance did a great deal to effect the masses that gathered to watch the flagellants. People began to put aside their differences with each other, criminals confessed their crimes and made amends, ursurs gave back ill gotten funds, and enemies became friends and many blood feuds were called off. As the processions moved on to the next town oftentimes a large number of people from each successive town would join the movement.

The flagellant processions had become a beacon of hope to the downtrodden and suffering masses of Europe. Soon the flagellants, as well as many of those who witnessed them, began to see themselves as not just working to absolve their own sins, but also the sins of others. Many of the flagellants believed that they were taking on the sins of the world and like Jesus were sacrificing their own bodies in order to save humankind. It was because of this that they were so accepted and loved by the masses of the towns and cities that they entered. They were given food, financial assistance, and always gained new members when they left.

In order to understand why these horrific processions were so successful one must look at the world in which they lived. Most of Europe's common people lived in harsh poverty. They were poorly clothed, starving, and constantly oppressed and harassed by the feudal state in which they lived. The Lords of the state demanded taxes and the Church demanded tithes, neither of which the peasants could pay and still be able to live and support their families. When wars would come the peasants had to support the armies that moved through the countries, and also suffered greatly when hostile forces would move upon their towns and villages. All to often the poor would be made to support one army, but not be given protection and then massacred by the next army.

The Church did little to help ease the suffering of the masses; in fact the Church was often seen as the enemy. Corrupt priests and clergy members took advantage of the laity as they disgraced women and burned "heretics", all the while demanding that each

person pay tithes. The commoners could not see how going to

church, receiving Holy Communion, and prayer were doing them

any good. Loyalty to the Church seemed to have gotten them

nowhere; it had even been harmful. Needless to say there was a

great deal of rage and dissatisfaction with the Church, and the

flagellants offered another way for the masses to touch God.

Sometimes the flagellant processions would take a more

revolutionary stance. When these revolutionary flagellants entered

cities they looted and burned churches, killed and tortured priests,

and preached against the Pope and the Church. These flagellants

claimed that they could attain salvation through their own efforts

and that they did not need the evil and corrupt Church to force

them into anything.

It was during this time of revolutionary flagellants that the

princes and bishops began to suppress the movements and burn

some of the leaders as heretics. By the late 1200's there were two distinct groups of flagellants. The church and state generally tolerated the processions in Italy and France, because they were more orthodox in their theology and not revolutionaries. However, the processions in Germany were ever increasingly fanatical and revolutionary. Many of these flagellant movements were met with violence and condemnation as heretics.

A part of the reason for the German condemnation of some of the revolutionary flagellants as revolutionaries was because of the mystical significance of the number thirty-three and one half. In some of the earlier flagellant movements the processions lasted for thirty-three and one half days, the supposed number of years which were spent by Jesus Christ on earth. This mystical number, combined with the fact that many of the flagellant leaders of the time claimed to possess Heavenly Letters, divinely inspired words from God, gave the church and state amble grounds and reason to condemn and destroy many of the revolutionary flagellant processions from the late 1200's to the late 1300's.

The outbreak of the Black Plague served to ignite many more flagellant processions throughout Europe. If the poverty and oppression were not enough, the Black Death made matters even worse. Once again, like their predecessors in 1260, the new flagellants took up their scourges and began to march. Like before, the flagellant processions gave hope to the people and the movement grew in power and numbers.

The flagellant movement died out in the 1480's as the last of the flagellants either stopped marching or were burned as heretics. Other than the suppression of revolutionaries, the flagellant movements died out for one major reason, disillusionment. After decades of marching and penance the world just did not get any better for anyone. The plague continued, the poverty continued, the oppression and the corruption of the church continued. The flagellants, without their knowledge, began to unwittingly spread the very plague they were trying to stop. Without any advanced knowledge of disease control or sanitation, they carried the sickness with them everywhere they went. Once a member of the procession contracted the plague, the rest of the group was sure to get it and then spread it to whatever town they came in contact with. The very nature of the flagellant processions was perfect for the spread of the plague, with their constant beating and bleeding bodies. Many of the flagellant groups had also gotten wrapped up in eschatology and believed themselves to be living in the endtimes. When the end never came, and they realized that what they were doing was not helping the situation, they could do nothing but lay down their scourges in defeat and go back home. They helped for a time, gave hope for a time, but in the end they could not make the changes they had sought to, a temporary solution to a very difficult and timeless situation.

A word on Demons

While no Christian will dispute the existence of demons, the aspects of their true nature, abilities, and presence is far from agreed upon. Though a minister I am not an expert on demonology or classical exorcism. I will not presume to lecture you on demons, though I will present the following statement, which is the extent of my opinion.

Demons are legion.

Demons are beings of, or at least permeated by, the energy of suffering. Thus, it is in their interest to propagate suffering, for it is either their fundamental essence or source of vitality.

Sin eaters do not banish, we consume.

An Open Letter to the Presiding Church Official

::Should you, the reader, find yourself being chastised for possessing this manuscript or have this manuscript confiscated, please turn to this portion and present this to your church official. This should resolve the situation.::

Dear Sir or Madam:

The general theme of this manuscript is the empowerment of Christians serving the Lord to their best ability, and is subversive only in that it calls into question the individual's sense of concrete reality and the boundaries of faith. By presenting sin eating as a tool and a way of life that can be used by a Christian in service of the Lord, it ceases to be a superstition or source of ambiguity and heresy. In short, this is a manual designed to help the minister use certain techniques to provide themselves and their bretheren with additional, if at times subtle or unorthodox, advantages in resolving the challenges of sin.

While this document does not espouse any particular denomination or dogma, it has been written with a certain group of Christians as the target audience. Given the growing denominational and spiritual diversity amongst the Christian faith, there are a large number of Christians who follow what can easily be dubbed "alternative" religious and spiritual paths. This document is a manual to help them reconcile their beliefs with their roles in the church and to empower them towards living their everyday lives.

The belief in the power of the sin eater on your part, or the congregation at large, is not required or relevant. Not to impune the importance of the insititutions of the Christian faith, however, it is the power of the belief of the individual sin eater that is of real importance. To illustrate, the mere act of observing subatomic particles can change them, so it is with the practice of sin eating.

Just like the power of prayer, the abilities of the sin eater are scientifically dubious at best, though in a very real and tangible way can affect the spiritual health of humanity. Even if it is not real, and who is to say that it is not, the faith and intensity invested by the sin eater is enough to change the world, even if at times the changes are only miniscule. A soul that is saved from damnation by the smallest of margins is still saved.

These people have a talent, a gift of will, belief, and power. It should be nurtured and encouraged, or at the least it should be free to flourish without interference. Let their talent be an asset, to themselves, their community, and the Christian faith. Capitalize on the advantage these talents provide, and there will be many challenges that cannot be overcome.

Regards,

Isaac DeLuca

About the Author:

Isaac DeLuca is a degreed theologian and practicing minister. Due to the possible controversial nature of this manuscript he prefers to take credit in name only, and has no intention of personal appearances or public speaking engagements relating to this work. However, he will gladly respond to questions via email and can be contacted at: IsaacDeLuca@hotmail.com

Notes & Contact Information

Made in the USA
San Bernardino, CA
18 October 2013